Advance Praise for *Our Birthright*

The Politics of Jesus for Black People Today

Keisha Krumm's voice is an essential voice crying out to the collective consciousness of the Black Evangelical church. Like Jesus of Nazareth, her work brings the good tidings of revolutionary radical thought and life affirming justice-anchored action.

This book is a love letter to Black evangelicals "to come out from among them," and it is a must read call to action for anyone interested in putting their love for God into the required Christian action of advancing God's kingdom.

Rev. Dr. Napoleon J. Harris V
Antioch Baptist Church
Cleveland, Ohio

As a revolutionary church, we embrace organizing for the purpose of fighting for justice, fighting against abusive powers, challenging authorities, pushing to initiate change, and empowering individuals to enact change.

Rev. Dr. Donna Childs
Tabernacle Community Baptist Church
Milwaukee, Wisconsin

Advance Praise for *Our Birthright*

The Politics of Jesus for Black People Today

Our Birthright is a bold and audacious literary manifestation of the heart and soul of a brave and courageous advocate for social justice.

The challenges that communities of color face today—especially with many conservative Evangelical churches questioning and even abandoning the Christian Church's fight for social justice—demand a reconsideration of the potential of Jesus' life-changing and social transforming ministry for the Black Church today.

The Bible studies in this book offer practical and insightful examples demonstrating Jesus' commitment to the poor and marginalized in society.

This is why Keisha Krumm has issued a clarion call to the Black Church and her voice cannot be silenced. My ministry and that of my church have been blessed because we heeded that passionate and prophetic voice. I recommend that all concerned give that voice serious consideration!

Rev. Dr. Demetrius K. Williams
Senior Pastor
Community Baptist Church
of Greater Milwaukee

OUR BIRTHRIGHT

The Politics of Jesus for Black People Today

Keisha Krumm

OUR BIRTHRIGHT

The Politics of Jesus for Black People Today
Keisha Krumm

Editing by Gregory F. Augustine Pierce
Text design and typesetting by Andrea Reider
Cover design by Betty Blexrud-Strigens + Midjourney
Author photograph by Dale McDonald,
   www.dalemcdonaldphotographer.com
Proofreading by Timothy Caldwell

Published by ACTA Publications, 7135 W. Keeney Street
Niles, IL 60714, (800) 397-2282, www.actapublications.com

ISBN: 978-0-87946-739-5

Printed in the U.S.A. by Total Printing Systems
Year 30 29 28 27 26 25 24 24
Printing 10 9 8 7 6 5 4 3 2 First
Text printed on 30% post-consumer recycled paper

CONTENTS

To my husband, Stuart.

To my mom, Johnnie Mae.

To my daughter, Olivia.

And to the Black Church.

May God's prophetic fire

burn in you

as we follow Jesus

the revolutionary.

INTRODUCTION

An Epiphany

I once had an epiphany. We had been struggling for five years to build a base of African-American churches and leaders to engage with institutions of other faiths (or groups with no proclaimed religious affiliation) in the organization I worked for at the time called Common Ground (CG). We had top Black pastors involved—such as Rev. Williams, Pastor Davis, and Rev. Taylor—but we did not have their members involved in the difficult work of fighting for justice that we were doing, and we needed them if we were going to truly succeed.

Common Ground at that point (2016) was already an organization with a track record: winning real change for people of Milwaukee with $33.8 million in reparations from five large banks, creating our own health insurance company, and getting Milwaukee Bucks owner Wes Eden's mortgage company, Nation Star, to invest $30 million in the city of Milwaukee for homeowners to refinance their mortgage and stay in their homes. Even with this strong track record, however, CG remained a predominantly white organization in a city that is predominantly Black and Latino. I was my job as the Leader Organizer to try to turn that around.

My epiphany came when I attended a meeting with leaders and organizers of the Metro Industrial Areas Foundation (IAF) in Baltimore in 2016. We organized a caucus of our black leaders and pastors to discuss their role in Metro IAF across the Great Lakes and Mid-Atlantic regions. As we were discussing the challenge of recruiting and growing the African-American presence in our organizations, one of the pastors said, "What we fail to understand is that Black folks are like white evangelicals when it comes to justice." Another pastor said, "Amen, I tell my people to tell your evangelical friends that Jesus and justice go together."

This discussion sparked an idea. If we were going to grow our base of African-American churches and lay leaders who are active in non-partisan political power organizing, I as a Black woman raised in the Black Church would have to learn to speak intelligently, passionately, and persuasively to the Milwaukee African-American evangelical churches' anticipated resistance of being "political" and discuss the historical context of Jesus of Nazareth and his revolutionary work of building the Kingdom of God. This is one of the many moments in my organizing work that I got to put my Master of Divinity degree to practice. That theological training helped me to develop a Bible study series that would be based in Scripture and credential organizing as the blessed work followers of Jesus are called to do in this world.

***

The Bible Study series was created and conducted in four Black churches in Milwaukee in 2017 and 2018 leading up to Common Grounds' ten-year anniversary convention.

With the help of Pastor Will Davis of Invisible Reality Ministries, I created material that would speak to his lay people and give them the confidence that working for justice is the work of the faithful. Pastor Will, Deacon Frank Finch III, Deacon Alex Hardy, and I formed the Common Ground Black Caucus to lead the way of getting the bible studies in the churches and working to develop an issue agenda that would speak to the African-American churches who were already members of Common Ground and prospective other religious and not-for-profit groups we were asking to join Common Ground.

This experience helped me reclaimed the revolutionary Jesus, strengthened my own faith, and reenforced my righteous indignation at the injustices that were being allowed—by billionaires, big business, corporations, politicians…or even inaction by the Black Church.

My journey of reclaiming my power as a follower of Jesus was a gift given to me, and now I am sharing it with you.

Keisha Krumm
Executive Director
Greater Cleveland Congregations
Juneteenth, 2024

Part 1

JESUS OF NAZARETH

"I see you're offing a class on the historical Jesus. I would like to sign up," I said. Professor Truex responded, "We will need to have a meeting to discern if your faith is mature enough to take this class. It's graduate level, and the content of the class will challenge and expand everything you've been taught about Jesus." Based on his response, I was even more intrigued. I replied, "Ok, let me know when we can meet to discuss." Professor Truex and I met, and after our thoughtful discussion I was approved to take the class. Professor Truex only admitted five students in this class. He was right, this class grounded and enlarged my understanding and faith in Jesus.

Growing up at New Salem Missionary Baptist Church in Wichita, Kansas, where the late Rev.

John L. Edwards was the pastor, I learned about Jesus Christ—the theological truth, the center of our tradition. We were taught that Jesus is the son of God. The truth of Jesus was the center of every sermon, Sunday school lesson, Bible study, and especially Easter Sunday. I Corinthians sums up these lessons perfectly: "For I handed down to you as of first importance what I also received, that Christ died for our sins according to the Scriptures, and that He was buried, and that He was raised on the third day according to the Scriptures" (15:3-4 [NASB]).

As I sat in the historical Jesus class at Tabor College in Hillsboro, Kansas, I learned that Jesus of Nazareth was Jewish. He was a unique historical figure who was politically conscious about the domination system that oppressed his people. He was shaped by the political, social, and economic situations of his time. He organized a political revolution he called "the Kingdom of God" and was crucified for it. Learning about Jesus of Nazareth spoke to me in new ways. I saw how he was shaped by his context and how his lived experience informed his actions. This understanding weaved together my faith and my wonder of Jesus Christ in new and powerful ways. It was this energy that helped me shape the Bible studies.

Let's start with Jesus' genealogy from the Gospel of Luke:

And Jesus himself, when he began to teach, was about thirty years of age, being the son (as was supposed) of **Joseph,** the son of Heli, the son of Matthat, the son of Levi, the son of Melchi, the son of Jannai, the son of **Joseph**, the son of Mattathias, the son of Amos, the son of Nahum, the son of Esli, the son of Naggai, the son of Maath, the son of Mattathias, the son of Semein, the son of Josech, the son of Joda, the son of Joanan, the son of Rhesa, the son of Zerubbabel, the son of Shealtiel, the son of Neri, the son of Melchi, the son of Addi, the son of Cosam, the son of Elmadam, the son of Er, the son of Jesus, the son of Eliezer, the son of Jorim, the son of Matthat, the son of Levi, the son of Symeon, the son of Judas, the son of Joseph, the son of Jonam, the son of Eliakim, the son of Melea, the son of Menna, the son of Mattatha, the son of **Nathan,** the son of **David,** the son of Jesse, the son of Obed, the son of **Boaz,** the son of Salmon, the son of Nahshon, the son of Amminadab, the son of Arni, the son of Hezron, the son of Perez, the son of Judah, the son of **Jacob**, the son of **Isaac**, the son of **Abraham,** the son of Terah, the son of Nahor, the son of Serug, the son of Reu, the son of Peleg, the son of Eber, the son of Shelah, the son of Cainan, the son of Arphaxad, the son of **Shem**, the son of **Noah**, the son of Lamech, the son of **Methuselah,** the son of **Enoch,** the son of Jared, the son of Mahalaleel, the son of Cainan, the son of Enos, the son of **Seth**, the son of **Adam**, the son of **God.**

(Luke 3:23-38, American Standard Version)

Luke's account of Jesus' genealogy is sometimes attributed to his mother Mary's family line along the male side. This is significant. Luke is making the point that Jesus is a descendant of King David through his *mother* and that his *father* is God. Thus, Jesus was both human and divine.

As Alex Haley reminded us in his book *Roots,* knowing where we come from is the beginning of knowing who we are. Jesus of Nazareth was rooted in the history of Israel and all humanity through the connection of Adam in his family tree. These accounts of Jesus' family history in Luke affirms Jesus' humanity and divinity.

Let's take a minute to reflect on this passage of Scripture:

- What names stick out to you? Why are some of them shown here in bold? (Hint: They all had a role in salvation history.)
- What do you remember about some of their stories? Why?
- Why do you think this list of names is important? What names would be on *your* genealogy list (literal or symbolic)?

The most interesting difference in the genealogy of Jesus in *Matthew's* gospel is the reference to four women, all mothers—Tamar (Genesis

38), Rahab (Joshua 2 and 6), Ruth (Ruth 1:16), Bathsheba (2 Samuel 11-12)—as significant in salvation history. (Kind of an unusual thing for a Jew like Matthew to do, especially at that time, don't you think?) Our focus in this Bible study, however, is not to look at the difference of the two stories but to investigate the central focus in both of them regarding Jesus in a historical context.

Let's shift to Jesus of Nazareth himself. We find narratives of the young Jesus in both Matthew and Luke that help us answer the question of who Jesus is and where he came from. Howard Thurman's book *Jesus and the Disinherited* has a useful interpretation of Jesus I find worthwhile and unique.

Thurman is a theologian. In 1949, he pastored one of the nation's first intentionally interracial congregations in San Francisco. He grappled with being a Christian because of his grandmother's experience of enslavement. He tells the story of her asking him to read the Bible to her, but she told him, "Do not read the Pauline texts the slave masters used to tell us to obey our masters." As an African-American man, a descendent of enslaved people, Thurman wrestled with the dominant image of Jesus created by Constantine, the first Christian Emperor of Rome in the fourth century AD. Thurman sought to find his way through an experience of Christianity that had been exercised as a dominant controlling force oppressing his people and others in the world. Yet, in the Black Prophetic tradition, he found a truth and a strength that forged his faith and theology. He is an incredible theologian.

To sum up in a sentence, Howard Thurman says, Jesus is for those who stand with their backs against the wall. In his interpretation of Jesus of Nazareth, he lays out a provocative interpretation of who Jesus was and who Jesus was not. Thurman reminds us:

- Jesus was a Jew of Palestine in the first century AD; he was not a Roman.
- Jesus was a poor Jew; he was not rich or wealthy.
- Jesus was a member of a minority group that lived under the dominant and controlling Roman Empire.
- Jesus was a human being organizing the building of the Kingdom of Heaven on Earth; he was not a detached celestial spirit.

Let's break each of these interpretations down and follow their implications for us today.

Jesus was a Jew. The people of Israel were God's chosen people; the people God chose to express his divine will, power, and creativity to the masses. Thurman says, "It is impossible for Jesus to be understood outside of the sense of community which the people of Israel held with God."

Jesus was a poor Jew. When the time came for the purification rites required by the Law of Moses, Joseph and Mary took him to Jerusalem to present him to the Lord (as it is written in the Law of the Lord, "Every firstborn male is to be consecrated to the Lord"), and to offer a sacrifice in keeping with what is said in the Law of the Lord: "a pair of doves or two young pigeons." (Luke 2:22-24)

Jesus' mother, Mary (Miryam), and his step-father, Joseph (Yosef), did not have the means to have a lamb so they brought two pigeons for the purification. The fact that Jesus (Yeshua) was poor put him in the boat with most of the people on Earth. Most people still are poor; we see this in our current time. Global economic inequality can be seen in the persistent and growing wealth gap that continues to expand. The world's twenty-six richest individual people own as much as the poorest 50% says Oxfam, the independent charity watch dog. The wealthiest 2000 people hold more wealth than the poorest 4.6 billion people combined. Thurman says that the fact that Jesus was a poor Jew makes him relevant to the oppressed, to the poor. This is not a point to labor on, but it has merit.

Jesus was a member of a minority group. He lived in the midst of a large dominant and controlling empire. In 63 BC, Palestine fell into hands of the Romans. The Jewish community lost their status, and their taxes were increased—not to fund their own Temple but to fund the building of temples that honored the Emperor Augustus Caesar. This is not unlike our current times, when for example we see the building of sports arenas with public dollars that increase the private gain of major sports owners by increasing the tax burden on local taxpayers.

When you live under domination and control, you ask the question: under what terms is survival possible? For Jews in Jesus' time, their physical bodies, their culture, and their faith were under attack. It's not unlike living while Black in the United States today. We saw this more specifically in 2020 from the deaths of George Floyd, who was publicly murdered by the police during an arrest after a store clerk suspected Floyd may have used a counterfeit $20 bill. And Breonna Taylor was fatally shot by police as she slept in her bed because the police had the wrong address. Their stories are just an example of the hundreds of daily experiences of Black people in this country. Or examples of Muslim brothers and sisters who are suspected of being terrorists because of their skin color, faith, or wearing a hijab.

Jesus lived under the dominant and controlling Roman Empire. In Jesus' time, when cities rose up against Roman dominance the people were taken siege and the cities were burnt to the ashes. This reminds me of the 1921 Greenwood, Oklahoma, massacre. Greenwood was an African-American town in Tulsa, Oklahoma. It was a town where African Americans were prospering. This fact did not sit well with surrounding white town folks. As a result, they killed hundreds of African Americans in a bloody riot, then burned down the town. The story was buried for 100 years, but recently it has come to light. My people are from Oklahoma, and my mom told me about this story before it became widely known, but she said the old folks would talk about it in whispers because it was too dangerous for the truth to come out because it might mean more death for our people.

Jesus was a human being, organizing the building of the Kingdom of Heaven on Earth, not a detached celestial spirit. In Reza Aslan's book *Zealot,* the author calls Jesus a Jewish revolutionary. In reading both Thurman and Aslan, I have put these two thoughts together in this phrase: Jesus was unique as a politically-conscious Jewish organizer. He was affected by the climate he grew up in. His people were under siege. They were not free. Thurman asks the question: What was Jesus' attitude toward Rome? Resist or not resist?

Different people in Jesus' time had different responses to Roman domination: Pharisees, members of a Jewish religious party that were prominent in Jesus' times, resented this system in silence and contempt; Zealots were a political movement that organized people to rebel against the Roman Empire, they took up arms and revolted. Jesus' response was to develop a different strategy by organizing a voluntary movement he called *The Kingdom of God.*

So Jesus was politically conscious. Herod, known as "Herod the Great," had a long reign in Jerusalem. He remolded the city, building magnificent structures of marble and gold. He was ruthless according to historians, and some call him "Herod the Monstrous." Early in his reign, he executed many of the Jewish aristocracy to establish his power and then took their land. Herod died in 4 A.D., but Rome continued his style of rulership through his sons, one who was also called Herod. The Temple became the center of the domination system in Jerusalem. Theologians John Dominic Crossan and Marcus Borg describe domination systems as structures that are ruled by the few, based on economic exploitation, who enjoy religious legitimization of their tyranny and abuse.

Jesus was politically conscious about the cruel system that ruled his people's lives. He was shaped by the political, social, and economic situation of his times. Jesus lived under such a domination system. Borg and Crossan explain the Roman system in their book *The Last Week:*

- **Political oppression.** A few ruled the many; ordinary people had no voice in the shaping of the society.
- **Economic exploitation.** Half to two-thirds of that society's wealth went to the hands of the wealthy and powerful. The wealthy élite created structures and laws about land ownership, taxation, slavery, and indentured labor.
- **Religious Legitimation.** The religious establishment developed language that legitimated and justified the laws and structure of domination.

This example from Jesus' time was not unlike Slavery, Reconstruction, Jim Crow, or the current attempts to subvert democracy in the United States. Our political system is based on race and color whenever and wherever African Americans and other people are oppressed. And religious language has been used in this country to legitimate the plantation economy and slavery. Laws were created and enforced to terrorize the formerly enslaved and demand their obedience in the system. This continues to this day.

Let's talk more about what it means to be *political.* In August 2021, Greater Cleveland Congregations was in a campaign called Battle for Democracy. This campaign focused on five congregations in five Cleveland neighborhoods. The work was to engage our neighbors in conversation about the November 2021 mayoral election. For the first time in sixteen years Clevelanders had an opportunity to pick a new mayor. We talked with our neighbors about their experience with COVID-19, inquired about their vaccination status, and asked them, "If you were elected mayor, what would be the first thing you would do when you get in office?" This question resulted in responses like, "You don't want to know what I think" to "The first thing I would do is get city services up to par and get all over-grown trees cut, fix the potholes in the streets, and create more activities for kids."

Yet we invited one potential new leader we met to come and canvass with us and bring any of the people she was already working with. She invited a young man named Aaron to attend. He came and experienced our canvassing. In our evaluation, he stood up and said, "I'm a Christian, and you all should be ashamed of yourselves, talking to people and asking them political questions like that."

So, what does it mean to be political? It simply means bringing the affairs of the city into public discussion and debate. This process tends to question the status quo. I will talk more about what it means to be political in session two. But it is clear to me that Jesus was a politically conscious Jewish revolutionary. He was engaged in promoting a movement he called *the kingdom of God:* "Now after John was arrested, Jesus came to Galilee, proclaiming the good news of God and saying the time is fulfilled, and the kingdom of God has come near; repent and believe in the good news." (Mark 1:14-15)

The concept of the kingdom of God is both political and religious. According to Crossan and Borg, "The Kingdom of God is a political as well as a religious metaphor. Religiously, it is the uppercase "Kingdom of God;" politically, it is the lowercase "kingdom of god." In the first century, *kingdom* was a political term. Jesus' hearers (and Mark's community) historically knew of and lived under kingdoms: Egypt, Babylon, the kingdoms of Herod and his sons, the Roman empire. Jesus could have spoken of the *community* of God or the *people* of God, but according to Mark and the other gospels, he always spoke of the *Kingdom* of God. To his hearers, Jesus' message would have suggested a very different kingdom from the domination systems that ruled their lives."

But Jesus' revolutionary message was watered down. Christianity became distanced from its Jewish roots and instead became rooted in Rome, the center of the most powerful empire in the world at the time, and in the process Jesus' revolutionary nature was tempered and softened.

Jesus saw and experienced what political oppression, economic exploitation, and religious legitimization was doing to his people. In response, he organized. He took a page from the prophet Jeremiah playbook as he challenged the temple and the priests for their theological legitimization of the domination system. He and his disciples created a popular movement with a new message, a new call, and a fresh challenge. This message gives courage to the oppressed, and Jesus' organizing challenged the oppression of his time and resulted in his execution.

Likewise, similar tempering of radical changemakers at one time reduced Rosa Parks to a woman who simply sat on a bus and refused to move because she was tired. This incorrect story downgraded Ms. Parks from her proper leadership role in a movement that focused on taking down the evils of segregation: Parks was in fact trained at the Highlander Folk School in New Market, Tennessee; civil rights organizers had failed in their attempts to address the issue of segregation on buses until they found the right leader. It was Rosa Parks.

History tried to temper the image of Rosa Parks (just as it has that of Jesus) because her *true* story was too radical and told a much more powerful narrative. I have seen how the watering down of radical action impacted my experience growing up in Wichita, Kansas. The only lesson we learned about Black people in my public-school education was Slavery. Today we see the challenge of teaching the truth about race and domination in the United States as it is plays out in local school boards, in suburban communities in Ohio, in the 2021 governor races in Virginia and New Jersey, in the presidential election of 2024. Dominant culture wants to tamper down the hard stories about white supremacy and the story of the African-American fight for recognition and identity in our national narrative.

This tendency to temper our politicalness, I believe, is why we don't learn about the revolutionary Jesus in our African-American churches. Knowing about Jesus as a political organizer creates a paradigm that causes us to examine the status quo and challenge the dominant power and culture. Once we have examined it, we are then called to act, to follow Jesus on the road of confronting the domination system. That road led to Jerusalem and Jesus' crucifixion.

As we move toward organizing in our local communities, let's remember that we are merely continuing the revolutionary work of Jesus: creating the Kingdom of God "on Earth, as it already is in Heaven."

QUESTIONS FOR REFLECTION AND DISCUSSION

1. Where are your grandparents and parents from? What forces brought you to where you are now? Why is it important to remember those stories?

2. Choose one or more of the following public events (or others not listed) that had a significant impact on you and/or your family and describe that impact. How is and will that impact be transmitted from your generation to the next?
   - American Slavery and Reconstruction
   - World War I
   - World War II/GI Bill
   - The Holocaust
   - Labor movement
   - Women's movement

- Civil Rights movement
- Black Power Movement
- The Great Depression
- The Korean or Vietnam War
- Suburbanization
- Changes in Public Education
- 2008 Recession and Foreclosure Crisis
- Black Lives Matter Movement
- Great Shutdown from the COVID-19 Pandemic
- The Big Lie and Attack on Democracy

3. Are you willing to learn about and then follow the revolutionary Jesus? Why or why not? If yes, how will you begin or continue to do so?

Part 2

RECLAIMING OUR BLACK POLITICAL BIRTHRIGHT

It was a cold fall day in Milwaukee, Wisconsin, in 2020. An NBA basketball star and a community organizer (me) were walking the streets of Milwaukee's north side with fifty Common Ground volunteers to get residents out to vote in the 2020 General election. I asked him, "When was the first time you voted?" He said, "I did not vote until 2008, when Barak Obama was running for President; until that point, I did not think voting mattered because I saw how Black people were treated by police, elected officials, and corporations. But in 2008, I saw my citizenship in new ways and decided to vote because I knew it would make a difference. Now today, I'm out here talking to neighborhood residents about the importance of voting because it matters." In 2008 this Black NBA basketball star claimed his political birthright, and in 2020 he took action to own it. His name is George Hill.

The Crown, a Netflix docuseries about the late Queen Elizabeth II, emphasizes the burden and blessings of birthrights. The series starts with King George VI, who stepped up to take the British crown when his brother, King Edward VIII, abdicated the throne in order to marry American divorcée Wallis Warfield Simpson. In the end, the stress of the crown and heavy smoking caused the early death of George VI.

The rest of the series shows how George's older daughter, Elizabeth, navigated the challenges, chores, and joys of the crown within her marriage, her relationships with her sister, and with her own children. In 2022, Queen Elizabeth II died at age 96, after the longest reign of any monarch in British history, and was replaced by her son, King Charles VIII. Her funeral and his coronation went on literally for weeks, covered wall-to-wall by British and world media (including in the United States).

For the British royal family, at least, political legacy matters.

As we look in the Bible at the story of the twin brothers, Jacob and Esau, Black people encounter the tension between the blessings and the burdens of birthrights. While the average person is not a king or queen, we all have birthrights that come with burdens and blessings. As African Americans who are descendents of enslaved people, navigating the burdens and blessings of our birthright requires work and commitment.

Here is a story from Genesis 25:29-34 in the New Revised Standard Version (NRSV):

Once when Jacob was cooking a stew, Esau came in from the field, and he was famished. Esau said to Jacob, "Let me eat some of that red stuff, for

I am famished!" (Therefore he was called *Edom* which means "Red.")

Jacob said, "First sell me your birthright."

Esau said, "I am about to die; of what use is a birthright to me?"

Jacob said, "Swear to me first."

So Esau swore to Jacob and sold his birthright to him.

Then Jacob gave Esau bread and lentil stew, and he ate and drank and rose and went his way.

Thus Esau despised his birthright.

In the Hebrew culture, Jacob knew that Esau cannot just give away his birthright, he had to *sell it* to him. Not only sell it but to *swear to sell it* to him. Esau in that moment, his stomach growling, smells the heavenly whiff of the stew and says, "What good is a birthright when I'm starving and going to die, what good is this birthright to me?" Hearing what Esau said, Jacob ups the ante and says that Esau must swear to exchange his birthright for a pot of stew.

Esau swore and sold his birthright. As promised, Jacob gave Esau the bowl of stew with bread, and Esau ate to his heart's content. When he was finished, he got up and left. The Scripture ends with saying Esau "despised" his birthright. In Hebrew, the word *despised* does not mean hated or loathed; it means regarded something as being of little concern or worth.

Let's get into Esau's head for a minute. Esau was out hunting and might not have been in a good headspace regarding family traditions. According to Jewish oral legend, finally written down in eighth century B.C. texts called *Midrash*, one thought is that Esau had been out shedding blood before the encounter with Jacob.

Rabbi Yehuda Altein, in his article *"Fourteen Facts about Esau Everyone Should Know,"* says, "Esau was out killing that day; he murdered Nimrod, who was a master hunter and was in possession of a cloak that had been passed down from Adam and attracted wildlife when worn, facilitating the wearer's hunting abilities, Esau strongly desired this cloak; so much that he plotted against Nimrod, murdering him and securing the cloak for his personal use. Maybe by the time Esau ran into his brother he felt that the cloak of Adam was much more powerful than the birthright he had received from their father Isaac."

But maybe there is another explanation. Esau the outdoorsmen was his father's favorite because he had a "taste for wild game" (Genesis 25:28). The Hebrew birthright is given to the oldest son, and according to biblical scholars, "The birthright includes double portion of the inheritance (Deuteronomy 21:17) and special ceremonial blessings from the father. Receiving the birthright from his father, the oldest son would become the head of the family, have charge of the family including the family property, and be responsible for the welfare of the younger sons, the widows, and any unmarried daughters. The oldest son was also to follow the religious line of the family and the connection to the temple."

But Esau seemed to be uninterested in this path of family responsibilities. He was an outdoorsman, a hunter, a murderer, and a thief, so the life of the temple was not for him. The birthright of carrying the seal of God through the family was not what he wanted.

Jacob, on the other hand, was a solitary or introspective soul who "sat in his tent and read." Genesis 25:27 says Jacob was a "plain" man. The Hebrew word for the adjective *plain* is translated elsewhere in the Scriptures as "perfect," "upright," "undefiled." Thus, the word *plain* referred to Jacob's character as a man of God. As a result, he would have been more interested in the family and religious responsibilities the oldest son was given to carry out than in the double portion of their father's inheritance. Perhaps Jacob's character gives some rationale as to why he went to such lengths to get Esau's birthright.

Esau, knowing his brother's temperament and interests, might have been happy to give up the responsibility of carrying the leadership responsibilities and religious rites of the family. After all, their story ends with Jacob becoming the bearer of God's plan for their family, and the two brothers eventually reconciled. (See Genesis 27-28.)

Do we give up our birthright for a bowl of stew? Sheldon S. Wolin, in his book *The Presence of the Past,* says the birthright we have given away to our present-day Jacobs is our politicalness. Wolin defines *politicalness* as our capacity for developing into beings who know and value what it means to participate in and be responsible for the care and improvement of our common and collective life.

Wolin says that, like Esau, "…our birthright is an inheritance. Like Esau's it's inherited from our fathers. Like Esau's it's a birthright that concerns a unique collective identity. Like Esau, our birthright is not being extracted from us by force, it is being negotiated or contracted away. Finally, like Esau, we have made it possible to contract away our birthright by forgetting its true nature and thereby preparing the way for its being reduced to a negotiable commodity with the result that its disappearance is not experienced as loss but as relief."

I resonate with what Sheldon Wolin is saying, and I think about my journey of owning my own birthright. I did not vote until I was twenty-seven; I did not think it mattered because the world I saw showed no real benefits for people who looked like me. I learned the gift I had as an African American from an immigrant named Socorro who had recently gained her American citizenship. She showed me my birthright in new ways.

Socorro told me this story when I asked her what things get her angry. She said, "I organized 300 Hispanic parents to fill our school library and got commitment from the local councilmen to attend the meeting. To my shock, Councilman Hector walked into the packed room and the first question out of his mouth was, 'Raise your hand if you can vote.' Three people raised their hands. Councilman Hector, yelled, 'Your kids can walk across the street on the broken sidewalks, or they can walk through the mud to get to school,' then he squared his shoulders turned his feet towards the door and walked out the overflowing room of Latino and Asian immigrants."

After she told me this story, I was outraged. But before I could get a word out, Socorro quickly said to me, "If that room was full Black people, he would not have asked that question." I was stunned by her response, because she knew that most Black people are citizens with the ability to vote; this agitated me to my core. As I reflected on the story she told me, I identified with the 297 people in the room who did not raise their hands because in the community where I grew up in Kansas, African Americans were treated like second-class citizens and many did not vote. As a working-class Black girl who went to public schools, wrestled with the strain of undiagnosed dyslexia, and saw my peoples' weathered dreams and worn-out spirits, everything had taught me that this country was not for me or people like me.

Socorro's simple question, however, pushed me in new ways to see the blood and sacrifice of Black people and to honor our freedom fighters—our forebears who had a will to be free and the courage to battle for voting rights, quality public schools for all, and to live where they wanted to live. Those forebears, including my mom and my grandmother, risked their lives, sacrificed everything so I would never be asked by some politician if I could vote.

In response to Socorro's story, I made a conscious choice then and there to own my birthright. I decided I would not be like Esau but rather embrace and celebrate and fight for my birthright. I registered to vote the next day and have done so in every election since.

***

Birthright is a mixed blessing. In order to not be like Esau, however, we Black folk have to grapple with the nature of our birthright, our inherited identity, and our obligation as African Americans to the common good. Wolin clarifies the work in these tasks. Our political inheritance or birthright is not something we acquire like sums of money or property when a family member dies, nor is it something we grow into without effort or forethought like when we reach the age of eighteen and automatically having the right to vote. We are entitled, but we must make it our own. Stir it in around our minds and knead it with our hands. Undertaking risks on its behalf and making sacrifices for it. Politicalness comes to us as a birthright, as an inheritance, and is defined by historical moments when identity is collectively established or reconstituted, according to Professor Wolin.

In the United States, we learn our history through wars beginning with the Revolutionary War, Civil War, World War I, World War II, Korea, Vietnam, Iraq, Afghanistan, and so on. My grandfather, Willie T. Shorty, taught me about a war I did not learn about in school, the Korean War. I learned how Grandpa Shorty put his body on the line. It showed in his mangled knee and his broken spirit because of the sacrifices he made for a country that threw him away and left him alone to deal with the memories of horrible war and the scars of his life of growing up in Memphis, Tennessee. When a birthright like his being inherited, we must decode the meaning it has for us today, and that meaning is wrapped up in our experience and the knowledge of the people who came before us.

Wolin says our collective political inheritance is a mixed blessing from foolish fathers. The African-American experience of actualizing full citizenship in our country is a journey of mixed blessings—full of good and evil, justice and injustice.

The history of the enslavement of our people was the first sign that claiming our birthright takes work to make the American birthright our own. Slavery was the beginning of a long line of policies and practices of this country that were set in place to devalue the birthright of people of color. We see this in the policies of the United States from redlining, a GI bill that cut off African Americans from generational wealth, Social Security discrimination against Blacks, and Roosevelt's unequal New Deal to name a few. Here are a few short analyses of what really happened.

***

The G.I. Bill was NFU (Never For Us). The Government Issue (G.I.) Bill after World War II gave returning veterans the ability to get loans, buy homes, and go to school. But when black men fought and died in the World War II and came home to be honored, they were instead cut out of the benefits of that bill and their sacrifices were ignored or, worse, seen as a threat to white supremacy in the United States. The G.I. Bill was "…racially discriminatory, as it was intended to accommodate Jim Crow laws. Due to the discrimination by local and state governments, as well as by private actors in housing and education, the G.I. bill failed to benefit African Americans as it did with white Americans," writes Erin Blakemore in his article, "How the G.I. Bill's Promise Was Denied to a Million Black WWII Veterans." While white veterans got settled and began to grow their families and build generational wealth, Black vets were thrust back into the world of Jim Crow.

For example, in 1947, only two of the more than 3,200 VA-guaranteed home loans in thirteen Mississippi cities went to Black borrowers. "These impediments were not confined to the South," notes historian Ira Katznelson. "In New York and the northern New Jersey suburbs, fewer than 100 of the 67,000 mortgages insured by the G.I. Bill supported home purchases by non-whites."

The original G.I. Bill ended in July 1956. By that time, nearly eight million World War II veterans had received education or training, and 4.3 million home loans worth $33 billion had been handed out. But most Black veterans had been left behind. As employment, college attendance, and wealth surged for whites, disparities with their Black counterparts not only continued but widened. There was, writes Katznelson, "…no greater instrument for widening an already huge racial gap in postwar America than the G.I. Bill."

Today, a stark wealth gap between Americans based on race persists. The median income for white households in 2019 was $76,057, according to the U.S. Census. For Black households it was $46,073, says Erin Blakemore.

Not only were they cut off from the benefits given to whites, but Black vets were also the target of mass lynching. According to the Equal Justice Initiative report, *Lynching in America: Targeting Black Veterans,* "No one was more at risk of experiencing violence and targeted racial terror than Black veterans who had proven their valor and courage as soldiers during the Civil War, World War I, and World War II. Because of their military service, Black veterans were seen as a particular threat to Jim Crow and racial subordination; thousands of Black veterans were assaulted, threatened, abused, or lynched following military service."

Was the New Deal a Bad Deal for Blacks? President Roosevelt's "New Deal" was a mixed bag of blessing and curses for African Americans. In Louis Menand's article "How the Deal Went Down," we learn that domestic workers and farm workers were excluded from Social Security in order to get white Southern Senators to vote for it. A majority of domestic and farm workers at the time were African American and Hispanic.

According to Larry Dewitt in his article "Decision to Exclude Agricultural and Domestic Workers from the 1935 Social Security Act," it's true that millions of Americans got a foothold into the middle class through the New Deal. But many of us today forget the crucial fact that black and brown workers across the country were systematically excluded from key programs like Social Security as well as protections afforded under the National Labor Relations Act. Also, the Homeowners Loan Corporation and the Federal Housing Administration promoted racial covenants and other instruments of segregation by refusing home loans for black and brown families.

According to a *Digital History* article, "African Americans and the New Deal," the New Deal did record a few gains in civil rights. Roosevelt named Mary McLeod Bethune, a black educator, to the advisory committee of the National Youth Administration (NYA). Thanks to her efforts, Blacks received a fair share of NYA funds. The WPA was colorblind, and Blacks in northern cities benefited from its work-relief programs. Harold Ickes, a strong supporter of civil rights who had several Black workers on his staff, poured federal funds into Black schools and hospitals in the South. Most Blacks appointed to New Deal posts, however, served in token positions as advisors on Black affairs. At best, they did manage to achieve a new visibility in government.

Was redlining a racist strategy, and was there no way around it? The practice of "redlining" was another government policy that created generational wealth gaps between those of different races and ethnic backgrounds. It demonstrates another example of the mixed bag of Black birthrights in this country.

Redlining was developed by the Homeowner's Loan Corporation. They created a map they called residential security maps. These maps were used to guide "responsible lending." Each map listed certain geographical areas as "hazardous for lending" and literally outlined these communities in red ink. These maps were then used to deny mortgages and services to people who lived in redlined neighborhoods, regardless of their creditworthiness, and thus destroyed predominately Black and other urban neighborhoods with a simple swipe of a pen.

In short, the middle decades of the twentieth century were an age of ghettoization. In his book *The Color of Law,* historian Richard Rothstein shows how and why this happened and proves that it wasn't by accident. Blacks did not simply move into overcrowded slums as a matter of group preference; nor was private racial discrimination by white developers, banks and homeowners' associations exclusively to blame, though it was certainly a key factor. Rather, the federal government used its expanding power to promote apartheid-like separation of whites and blacks in cities and towns across the country. (A recent four-part documentary directed by filmmaker Bruce Orenstein titled *Shame of Chicago, Shame of a Nation* lays bare the true stories behind how Chicago and its suburbs helped devise the nation's most sweeping system of racially segregated communities and how these policies diminished the lives of generations of Black families, creating the vast racial wealth gap that persists to this day.)

Homeownership was a key path to wealth in postwar America, yet many Blacks were excluded. Today, the median white household's net worth is sixteen times that of the median African-American household, writes Rothstein.

Why did our resilience never wane? During these struggles, and countless others, Black people proved we are resilient. "We bend, we don't break. We sway!" sings the chorus in the second act of Terence Blanchard's musical *Fire Shut Up in My Bones.*

We did not bend or break. We developed deep roots in the Black family, Black church, Black communities, and Black institutions like the NAACP, SNCC, and Historically Black Colleges and Universities (HBCUs) during the onslaught. They uncovered the strategies that were developed to keep our people as a permanent underclass. Working to gain and own the rights of citizenship of this country shows the true grit of our people that continues to this day.

Throughout history, we used the tool of power organizing to right wrongs done to our communities. In Milwaukee, Common Ground, a powerful nonpartisan political multi-racial organization, created the Milwaukee Rising campaign that leveraged $33M from US Bank, Bank of America,

Deutsche Bank, and Chase Bank to restore the damage redlining created in the Sherman Park community of Milwaukee during the 2008 sub-prime mortgage scheme. Sherman Park is majority African American. The work of Common Ground was the catalyst to putting African Americans in homes, stabilizing entire blocks, and addressing other issues in that community. This is another example of how through organizing we reclaim our political birthright and right wrongs that were intended to destroy our communities.

Today in Washington, DC, WIN (Washington Interfaith Network) is fighting to create Black equity through homeownership. This campaign has leveraged significant public dollars to right the wrongs of redlining and systemic racist policies that encouraged and subsidized homeownership for white Americans and not for disadvantaged people of color, especially Black Americans, in the DC area. WIN pressured the Mayor of DC to create a $10M fund for Black Home Ownership for first-time home buyers, and WIN continues the movement to own their political inheritance.

Was *the* Declaration of Independence *our* Declaration of Independence? Grappling with the history and the intentionality of polices aimed at destruction of black communities and families, it's hard to not be like Esau and "despise" our political birthrights. In my journey of reclaiming my own political birthright, I have learned that it takes work and commitment for me to continually reinterpret the value of Blacks' birthrights in this country and find ways—as did our ancestors before us—to value, own, and fight for our birthright on this land.

Dr. Danielle Allen, a professor of political philosophy, ethics, and public policy at Harvard University and director of Harvard's Allen Lab for Democracy Renovation, takes a unique look at the Declaration of Independence in her book *Our Declaration.* In a sense, her book is her effort to reinterpret the founding document of our nation and the meaning it has for her and us today.

Dr. Allen chose the Declaration of Independence as she was teaching a night class at the University of Chicago for adults who were living in poverty and working dead-end low-wage jobs while finding creative ways to find childcare, do meaningful work, and better themselves by attending a college course. As she wrestled with creating a high-quality educational experience for people on the go who do not have a lot of time to sit down and read a book, she decided to use the Declaration of Independence for one of the reading assignments because it is both well written and short.

Dr. Allen's experience of teaching this founding document created an experience where people learned in new ways about the Declaration of Independence. She also saw the journey of her students as they grappled with the mixed bag of their political birthright. Her students, like many of us, thought that the Declaration of Independence was meant for white men or white people, but not for African-Americans, immigrants, and other people of color. Dr. Allen dared to ask them the question: Is the Declaration of Independence for you? After asking the question she created an experience for them to answer that question with their eyes wide open.

Yes, it's our Declaration. Whose did you think it was? I asked this question to a group of leaders who attended an organizing training I conducted at Lee Road Baptist Church in the Lee Harvard neighborhood of Cleveland, Ohio.

Lee Harvard is a neighborhood once known as a "suburb in the city." It was a middle-class Black neighborhood full of residents who worked as postal workers, city workers, federal employees, auto workers, factory workers, and healthcare workers. The dynamic of having living-wage middle-class jobs created the opportunity for Black people to own homes and build community. Today this neighborhood has been coined as a "Middle Neighborhood" by the city of Cleveland. It does not have the shine and luster of its former days, but it has a base of resilient and dedicated residents and institutions that are committed to doing the hard work of stabilizing their community and bringing rejuvenation.

The training had people who were in their sixties or older. When I asked them if the Declaration of Independence was meant for you, half of them answered "no" and half answered "yes." One individual who answered negatively replied, "We were slaves when it was written; would you write something for all the broken washing machines you have in your yard?" An individual who responded positively responded, "If I look at it today, I say yes, it is for us; I had my grandson read it."

Dr. Allen says, "Yes, the Declaration is for us." She goes on to say that the brilliance of this document is that it tackles two key questions about human agency and organizing the powers of government to secure and protect our individual and collective right of life, liberty, and the pursuit of happiness. The Declaration of Independence was written in a time when the thirteen colonies were being oppressed by Great Britain. These colonies were seeking to be free of oppression and wanted the ability to chart a new way forward. To be free from Great Britain and her kings and queens, the founding fathers had to persuade those living on farms and in towns in the colonies to take up arms against Great Britain and fight to create the United States of America.

Take that, Elizabeth II and Charles III.

Is the Declaration tainted by its authors? When we ask the question if the Declaration of Independence is for Black people and we say no, it's because we miss the contribution of people like John and Abigail Adams to the Declaration of Independence. Dr. Allen says that the Declaration of Independence is attributed to Thomas Jefferson, a slave owner, because he was the chair of the committee and they dubbed him the "writer of the Declaration of Independence." But Dr. Allen jokes, "If you want to claim you did something, put it on your tombstone. It won't be refuted." She points out that John Adams was chair of five committees and on the team of the five people who drafted the Declaration of Independence. He was an abolitionist, never owned slaves, and made important contributions in the Declaration that set a foundation of equality. And his wife, Abigail Adams, was his primary collaborator in all his political endeavors throughout his life—including being the second First Lady of the United States. "Don't forget the ladies," she once chided her husband.

The second reason some Blacks think the Declaration is not for us is that we miss three important compromises that were made that defend equality: that ALL people are created Equal; that they are ALL endowed by their Creator with certain inalienable rights; and that the three most important rights they are ALL entitled to are: "Life, Liberty, and the Pursuit of Happiness."

<hr>

All people are created equal. That means "equal" needs to be unpacked. According to Dr. Allen, the wording of "separate and equal" meant that the thirteen colonies were separate from Great Britain, equal as a world power, and free from domination. Equal, in other words, as countries like England, Spain, France, and others, and capable of making decisions for themselves and organizing their shared lives.

Dr. Allen says, if we read the full context of the Declaration of Independence, we see that the founders meant all people, thus she rewrites the sentence as, "All *people* are created equal," not just white men with property. This included enslaved individuals (and this understanding was used by abolitionists who fought to end slavery). We see it most specifically in the case of a Black man named Prince Hall, who was born enslaved and gained his freedom shortly after the Revolutionary War. In 1777, Hall petitioned the State of Massachusetts to abolish slavery based on the promise of liberty discussed in the Declaration of Independence. He won that petition, and Massachusetts became the first state to end slavery.

On the issue of gender, the Declaration of Independence says that women are equal to men but that men will run the government and shape it. This notion was challenged from the beginning by women, but it was not until 1920 that white women earned the right to vote. It took another five decades for Black women to fully benefit from the 19th amendment that made it legal for all women to vote. "Don't forget the ladies," indeed!

Are Black people endowed with rights that are "inalienable"? We are endowed with these rights, but the text makes a compromise by using the word "Creator," which is a nod toward both the religious and the secular. It also leans towards politics. Dr. Allen says, "Human beings have been born with powers of mind, spirit, and body to live, be free, and pursue happiness. Because politics comes as naturally to human beings as living, being free, and pursuing happiness, politics is the tool nature has developed to protect those fundamental human powers."

Perhaps one of the most significant phrases in the Declaration of Independence that lends itself to equality is the statement, "That among these are Life, Liberty, and the Pursuit of Happiness." Dr. Allen tells us that John Adams inserted the phrase "pursuit of happiness" and removed the phrase "pursuit of property." This phrase was a win for the anti-slavery movement. Including the phrase *pursuit of happiness* was a direct statement of the commitment to end slavery at some point in the future of the developing nation.

The Declaration of Independence became the foundation of the antislavery movement, which history also calls the "abolitionist movement." This movement was making progress and slavery was on its way out, but then came the invention of the cotton gin. This machine crystalized the economics of slavery in a new way and the enslavement of African people became an intrenched necessity for the economy of the South. The entrenchment of this economy led to the Civil War, where North and South fought over the tension inherent in our founding documents and institution of slavery. This war ended with the Emancipation Proclamation and the creation of the 13th amendment outlawing slavery, the 14th amendment giving citizenship rights to all people born in U.S., and the 15th amendment giving Black men the right to vote. These amendments ushered in a new day for freed enslaved people that scholars call the "Black Reconstruction"—a period when Blacks began to prosper, rebuild, and run for and hold public office.

This Black Reconstruction stage ended with the Compromise of 1877, which ushered in Jim Crow laws. These local laws generated so-called "separate-but-equal" regulations that segregated every aspect of society from water fountains to bathrooms to buses to neighborhoods to schools, to name a few. The segregationists in effect changed the language of the Declaration of Independence from "separate and equal" to "separate but equal" to keep African Americans, Mexicans, Chinese, Indigenous Peoples, and anyone else not "white" subjugated and dependent.

Jim Crow (1877-1964) was initially whittled away by the Supreme Court decision in 1954 Brown v. Board of Education of Topeka, Kansas, ending racial segregation in public schools, and it ended with the 1964 Civil Rights Act that outlawed discrimination based on race, color, religion, gender, and national origin. The 1965 Voter Rights Act outlawed race discrimination in voting and has been used to uphold equal voting rights for voters of color.

Yet today, these protections are being intentionally attacked, and Black people need to continue to claim our political birthright because we need it more than ever. In this country and around our world, African Americans and other ethnic minorities have borne the brunt in recent years of a global financial crisis and a pandemic-driven global downturn. Many of us are growing pessimistic about our long-term economic future and losing confidence in democracy itself. We cannot let that happen. It would be selling our birthright for a bowl of stew.

***

So, are there any good signs of hope? We see one in Cleveland, though while voter registration goes up voter turnout goes down. The Greater Cleveland Congregations (GCC) has coined the phrase *voter depression* to describe what's happening with voters. Through our conversations at people's doors, we know that voters are concerned about the state of their communities and care about making their local neighborhoods better, but they do not trust elected officials to make the changes they want to see to improve their communities.

Many voters do not see how voting in local or general elections makes a difference.

GCC has created a multiple-year strategy called "Battle for Democracy" to increase voter turnout in five neighborhoods in Cleveland by connecting democracy to on-the-ground non-partisan local power organizing. Through our work, GCC member organizations are going out and building relationships with residents who live around their buildings. They talk with, listen to, and design issue campaigns that put the concerns of the people before local elected officials in a way that compels them to hear and act on the changes we demand. After elections, we hold decision makers accountable to make the changes our leaders and residents have called for.

We have seen examples of positive movement with our campaign to open a local pool in Fairfax neighborhood or listening to residents in Lee Harvard neighborhood about getting an intergenerational park. We reach out to thousands of voters every election and provide nonpartisan information for them to exercise their right to vote and provide local actions for residents to shape and engage with decision makers. In the second year of our work, during the 2021 local election, we saw an 8% increase of voter turnout by voters contacted by GCC, according to a Union of Concerned Scientists Fellow, Dr. Michael Latner.

Those who have checked out of our democracy or think it is worthless depend on us to show a different way, as Professor Allen did with her students or as GCC does in organizing Black churches. We Blacks can claim and own our democracy. Our founding documents are for all of us and they call us to continue to do the work it takes to make our birthright ours. Sociologist Sheldon Wolin calls this work our "politicalness," our capacity for developing into beings who know and value what it means to participate in and be responsible for the care and improvement of our common and collective lives.

QUESTIONS FOR REFLECTION AND DISCUSSION

1. Have you or someone you know well ever been tempted to disregard or disdain a birthright? Tell the story.

2. How will you make sure your birthright remains yours and is not sold for a bowl of stew? Be specific about what you plan to do, both individually and through your church.

3. Have you ever voted? If so, how many times? When did you first vote? Why did you choose that moment to vote? What have been the results of your voting for you and for the common good?

Part 3

NO POWER =
NO JUSTICE

The fortunes of my family changed when I was in sixth grade, because my mom got a job at Boeing's plant in Wichita, Kansas, joined the local union, and found a church home. Mom was hired as one of only two African Americans to inspect airplane parts, which was a great job.

The year was 1985, and Easter Sunday was near. Mom took my brother and me shopping to Dillard's, an upscale department store chain, to buy new Easter outfits. This was unusual for our family. Before my mom's union job, we put our clothes on lay away, paying no interest and picking it up later when we could pay the balance. We shopped at K-Mart, the pioneer of discount retail.

But with Mom's new job, she was able to buy my brother, me, and herself new Easter Sunday outfits. My brother got a suit and tie, he looked so cute. I received the best outfit ever: a pink skirt; a pink, white and blue blouse; a pink sweater; all topped off with pink shoes and pink stockings! My mom bought herself a new outfit as well, so we were a well-dressed and good-looking family. My outfit must have cost her $90 back then. When we walked into church that Sunday, we looked as good as we felt. I remember the joy that radiated from my mom and the smile she had on her face because, as our family's primary bread winner, she was finally able to provide for us the way she had always dreamed. That afternoon when we got home, we topped off the joyous experience with a feast made for kings and queens.

My mother's living wage gave her the ability to provide a decent standard of living for her and our family. In addition to her having the ability to pay for food, water, housing, and transportation, she also got health and dental insurance that allowed her to cancel our public assistance help. Years later, I was able to get braces. Mom was able to attend my basketball games and track meets and be home in the evening to help us with our homework. She also joined the church choir and started a youth group. I learned that a living-wage job is a must for family stability. We were proud members of New Salem Missionary Baptist Church, and Mom was an active dues-paying member of the United Auto Workers, who represent Auto and Aerospace workers to this day.

This chapter contains the key concepts I have learned since then. They all add up to "No power equals no justice."

CHARITY AND JUSTICE

In the Summer of 2017, Tabernacle Baptist Church members conducted a neighborhood "walk-to-talk" with our neighbors. Tabernacle is in the 53206 zip code. A 2015 film documentary, *Milwaukee 53206,* maintained that 53206 is "the most incarcerated zip code in the nation." Meaning a majority of its men have spent time in jail or prison. As the members walked and talked with neighbors, we introduced ourselves, asking our neighbors "What are the pressures facing your family?" We heard stories about drug houses, abandoned houses, the challenge of finding quality public education, and the need for jobs that enabled residents to successfully take care of their families instead of working two or three jobs that barely made ends meet.

When we reconvened the following week to reflect on the experience. I asked our members, "What is your response to the stories we heard and the things we saw?" Some said, "We need to keep doing our food bank." Others said, "We need to get more people to our community garden."

As the then lead organizer for an organization called "Common Ground" in Milwaukee, I responded, "Yes, the immediate response of seeing these needs is more charity and continuing to provide more food and clothing to the community." But then I said, "And we must also organize for justice."

This is the point of this little book: The response of justice is to think about how we can move beyond charity and service to build the power we need to impact the pressures on families in a way that allows people to do for themselves and their family what my mom did for her family thirty years earlier in 1985.

When some Black congregations see overwhelming needs in their communities, often their first response is charity. A good definition of church charity might be: *acts of providing food, shelter, and clothing to individuals in our communities who are in need, through services or programs.* Perhaps the more challenging response for many Black congregations is justice. Justice for churches is *the work of focusing on the root cause of the lack of food, shelter, or clothing in our communities.* The work of doing justice calls us to step back and analyze what our neighbors are experiencing and why, asking questions that identify actors who are causing the abandoned houses, drug activity, or loss of jobs. Asking ourselves, what are the common themes we are hearing from our conversations? Is there only a handful of people who have this specific need or is it a real societal problem? How can we be present to our neighbors and work together to change the public policy or law that is creating the condition? What kind of power do we need to create a new solution or effect change for hundreds or thousands of people impacted? The answer, at least for Christians, is found in this Bible passage:

Seek the welfare of the city where I have sent you into exile, and pray to the LORD on its behalf; for in its welfare you will have welfare."

Jeremiah 29:7 (New American Standard Bible)

After reading several translations of Jeremiah 29:7, I settled on the one from the New Revised Standard Bible version above, "Seek the welfare of the city," instead of the King James Version that says, "Seek the peace of the city," because the English word *peace* has become so watered down in the last four hundred years since King James sponsored his translation. The Hebrew word for peace is *shalom*. The meaning of *shalom* goes farther than peace. It means wholeness and health. *Shalom* refers to the internal peace we have in our soul, spirit, and body.

But *shalom* is even more than that. It applies to our relationships at work, at home, in our neighborhoods, and in our relationship with nature and creation. "To have *shalom* is to be whole and healthy in yourself and in all that challenges you, be it people, be it the issues of your world, your environment, your society, or be it the problems which are at hand, the problems which await you," said theologian Walter Brueggemann.

POWER TO GRIEVE

In our current context in the United States of America, I believe a critical focus of our time and energy as the Black church is to seek the welfare of the city, our neighborhoods, and our people. In order to seek the welfare of the city, we must have power to file grievances to make our communities whole. If we are interested in moving toward wholeness and well-being, having a strong emphasis on justice-seeking and not allowing ourselves to be lulled by the harmony of charity has a chance of getting us closer to building better communities.

I was able to spend one and a half years as a union organizer for health care workers in Washington State with the Service Employees International

Union (SEIU). As a union organizer, I learned a lot about the grievance process. Labor unions negotiate contracts with employers. These contracts include worker standards, pay, working conditions, vacation, sick leave, retirement, etc. When a contract is broken or violated, the member has the *right* to file a grievance, to seek a remedy that will make the member whole *according to the contract.*

It's interesting to me that a grievance is remedied only when someone is made whole. For a worker to be made whole, however, he or she has to belong to a labor union that has the power to form a union, negotiate with the employer to get a contract, and enforce the contract when it's broken.

In organizing people for power, we believe that if we are to move toward wholeness we need institutions that have enough recognition and respect to negotiate and to win agreements from others who wield power over us. One example in 2023 was how two best friends, Christian Smalls and Derrick Palmer, were able to organize current Amazon workers inside and outside their workplace to build relationships and trust with workers, including supporting those who got fired by Amazon for their organizing work. The two Black men organized for eleven months, and the workers won a union election to form the Amazon Labor Union at the JFK8 Fulfillment Center on Staten Island, which became the first American Amazon warehouse to have its workers win a union election. Having a union will give the workers the power to negotiate better conditions with Amazon. June 18, 2024, Amazon Labor Union members voted to affiliate with the International Brotherhood of Teamsters. The Teamsters are 1.3 million members strong and one of the largest labor unions in the country. I have no doubt the Teamsters will fight with all their might to make sure these unionized workers secure a union contract with Amazon.

POWER

I think the number-one issue facing Black communities is the lack of the *power to organize* to make a more just world. To some, *power* is a loaded word full of bad experiences and negative images. In our work, organizers talk a lot about power because we know that to organize to create a more just world we simply must have power. We in the Black churches must reclaim the word *power* and think about how we use it together to make our communities and workplaces be for everyone—not just big business, billionaires, and politicians.

The most basic definition of power is "the ability to act," Dr. Martin Luther King, Jr., said. "Power without love is reckless and abusive, and love without power is sentimental and anemic. Power at its best is love implementing the demands of justice, and justice at its best is power correcting everything that stands against love."

In English, when we talk about power or even look it up in the dictionary, the first definition listed is a noun. We talk about power as if it's a person, a place, or a thing. We talk about power as if it is something we possess and hold in our hand. If it is shared, we think, then the power is lost. Power is often treated like the ring of power in J.R.R Tolkien's novel *The Lord of the Rings*. There could only be one Lord of the Rings, only one person could have and hold it. It could not be shared. The ring was a *thing* to possess and to covet.

In Spanish, however, the word *power* is *poder;* it is a *verb* that means "can or to be able to." Power is an action, not a thing you possess. We can *poder* well or *poder* badly, but there is a choice of how we *use our* power.

As Black people of faith, we believe that we are all given power. 2 Timothy 1:7 says, "God has not given us the spirit of fear, but of power and love and a sound mind." Power is innate, we are born with it, and we are called to use it to make the world better for what Jesus called "the least of these"—those left behind and those shut out.

I see this most clearly in my daughter. When she was four years old, we drove from Milwaukee to Kansas to visit my mom. It was a twelve-hour drive. I made several busy bags for Olivia so she would be occupied on this long drive. I put fun items like play dough, blocks, paper, tape, children's scissors, markers, crayons, and window clings to name a few. She enjoyed the busy bags, and we made it to Wichita without a meltdown! It was a proud-mom moment. We got to my mom's, cleaned out the car, then loaded it up a few days later to go visit Olivia's cousins. As I was buckling her in her car seat, I noticed the seatbelt was cut. So I moved her to the other side, that seatbelt was half cut! I was in shock and not happy. I said, "Hey, Olivia, what happened to the seat belts?" She said, "I don't know, Mommy." I asked her, "Olivia, did you cut them with the scissors?" She finally admitted, "Yes, I wanted to see what would happen."

I busted up laughing. My daughter had been doing a science experiment! In that moment when she was buckled in for a long drive, she had realized she had power. She had the ability to experiment with her ability to cut a seat belt. After I laughed for a while, we talked about how scissors are for paper or tape not for seat belts. I too learned my lesson: Keep scissors out of busy bags. But I was still proud of her.

Power is in all of us. It is the ability to act. We get to decide how we use *our* power. Our children know this early in their lives, but sometimes we drum it out of them.

As we work to create a more just world, let's remember we all need to build power to get more justice, and we have to organize for power if we want justice.

***

POWER, ECONOMICS, AND WEALTH

I dare to say that Black people are duty-bound to understand power. Who has it and why; how do they use it, and for what purpose? Former U. S. Secretary of Labor, Robert Reich, writes, "Power is the ability to direct or influence the behavior of others. On a large scale, power is the capacity to set the public agenda, to frame big choices, to influence legislators, and to get laws enacted or prevent from being enacted, to assert one's will on the world."

It is widely regarded that our economy is rigged to benefit big business and billionaires and some politicians. Reich's book *The System, Who Rigged It, How We Fix It,* has a clear analysis of how power and political economics works in our country. Reich was President Clinton's Secretary of Labor. When he was in the President's cabinet, he saw several policy changes that laid the groundwork for the pain of what Black people—and almost all people—are experiencing today. He warned that our government would be releasing a monster if it changed the Glass Stegall Act, a long-standing federal law that put some limits on Wall Street. In 1999, however, Glass Stegall was repealed (during the Clinton Administration no less). We saw one of the impacts of this repeal in 2008 when the sub-prime mortgage schemers destroyed families and neighborhoods while big investors got wealthier. And not one of them went to jail.

I think Reich has a useful analysis about power and our economy and how it has impacted Black families and the average American. From my per-spective, far too many Black clergy have removed people power from sermons on Sunday morning and from Bible studies on Wednesday. It also seems in most high school and college classrooms, we have removed people-power from standard economic texts, finance courses, and even political science and law. Yet I believe we cannot wrap our heads around today's system without confronting our lack of power head on.

Reich explains that "Power is exercised through institutions like big Wall Street, the Federal Reserve, the Supreme Court, the military, elite universities, and the media (including social media as organized by big tech such as Google and Facebook). These institutions do not wield power on their own. Certain people have outsized influence over them, people such as the CEO of JP Morgan Chase, Jamie Dimon; large investors such as Warren Buffett; hedge fund managers such as George Soros; private equity managers such as Goldman Sachs; key lobbying groups such as the Business Roundtable (a nonprofit lobbyist association based in Washington, D.C., made up of CEOs of major US companies); and major donors not only to political candidates but also to colleges and universities (including HBCUs)."

To grasp the influence these decision makers have on our daily lives, in my view, Black people have an obligation to understand the role wealth plays. Reich suggests: "In the economic and political system we live in today, wealth and power are inseparable. Great wealth flows from great power;

great power depends on great wealth; and, as a result, wealth, and power have become one in the same."

Reich continues to say, "Three decades after World War Two, we saw a growing middle class, a steadily more inclusive democracy, a nation grappling with problems like poverty, inequality of opportunity, and environmental decay: African Americans' push for Civil Rights gained speed and results. Many Black people had steady jobs in factories and manufacturing. Milwaukee, Cleveland, and Chicago boomed during these times as African Americans journeyed North in the Great Margination."

I remember hearing stories in my individual meetings in Milwaukee from older Black men who said, "I could start a job in the morning, quit that job at lunch, then after lunch I could go get a new job." Jobs were plentiful and they paid enough for Black people to buy homes, take care of their family's needs, and have enough to take a nice vacation. "This balance relied on strong unions, a government willing to regulate corporations, and large corporations rooted in their communities and responsible for the well-being of their employees, neighbors, and stockholders," writes Reich.

"In the last forty years, the opposite has occurred; the middle class has shrunk and democracy itself is under attack. Power has concentrated in the hands of the few, and those few have grabbed nearly all the economic gains for themselves," he argues.

MEDIATING COMMUNITIES

Thucydides, an ancient Greek historian, said, "You only get as much justice as you have the power to compel. The truth about power is the strong do what they have the power to do and the weak accept what they must accept." Organizing for decades, I can see this is true.

A common quote I hear that paints this picture goes somewhat like this: "If you're not at the table, you are on the menu," or "If our interest is not represented at the decision-making tables, we are put in a financially vulnerable position and could be left out, or worse be on the menu to be served."

As Black congregations expand their mindset to include a paradigm of justice, I think it calls us to think of each Black church as a mediating community that organizes for justice and builds power to give families a fighting chance. An interesting insight of modern social thought is the importance of *mediating communities*, a term coined by my friend and mentor Richard (Dick) Harmon, a recently deceased Industrial Areas Foundation theorist and organizer, as he examined how institutions are in decline and the places where people are now finding support and agency to move and act with power.

Mediating communities include churches, schools, fraternal organizations, professional associations, neighborhood associations, block clubs, and even social clubs! Mediating communities are all the places where people volunteer their time out of a sense of values. They are a place where people go to have the world explained to them or to make sense of where they live in it. Mediating communities have membership, mission, and money. Black churches should be mediating communities.

Greater Cleveland Congregations (GCC), for which I now work, has organized thirty-nine congregations and nonprofits to build a powerful organization that can leverage significant justice in the Greater Cleveland communities and local neighborhoods. GCC worked with former republican Governor John Kasich to get Medicaid expansion for thousands of people in Ohio. GCC worked with Cleveland Metropolitan School District to successfully pass three levies in 2012, 2016, 2020 that invested over $900M in public education for Cleveland children. This public investment in Cleveland children aided the Cleveland Public School to become the number-one urban public school district in the state in 2022. GCC stepped in the gap, organized power, and leveraged wins that changed the lives of thousands of families throughout Cleveland and Ohio. This is an example of what can happen when congregations pool their power. Big change results when we make life better for families and relieve some of the pressure they are facing.

Mediating communities have the opportunity to stand between families and the dominant power structure. And to be places where families go when they are dealing with the pressures the dominant power system is placing on them.

ORGANIZED PEOPLE AND ORGANIZED MONEY

We organizers teach that power comes in two forms: organized people and organized money. Two examples of organized people power are Montgomery Bus Boycott and GCC's Color of Health Initiative.

Growing up, the common story I heard about Rosa Parks was that she got on the bus in Montgomery, Alabama one day after a long day of work. She was tired. Her feet hurt, so she refused to give up her seat to a white man. I did not learn until I was in my early thirties that this was not the true story: It described Parks as a tired individual, acting alone, removed from the power of the organized money and organized people that executed the first large scale demonstration against segregation that lasted for 382 days. I think the "tired feet" story of Rosa Parks buries the genius of the organizing strategy and power of the Black church.

The Montgomery Bus Boycott was led by leaders who were trained and organized through their Black congregations and community organizations. The roots of this work were started by the Women's Political Council (WPC), a group of professional black women started in 1946. There had been other attempts to desegregate bussing in the south, but the calculus changed only when Rosa Parks was arrested. She had been active reorganizing the local NAACP and had a reputation of being a fighter; she was well-known and respected, and the community knew she would not flinch under the pressure that would be brought on her from being arrested.

Ms. Parks was trained. According to biographer Jeanne Theoharis' book, *The Rebellious Life of Mrs. Rosa Parks.* "Five months before Rosa makes the stand on the bus, she goes to Highlander Folk School in Tennessee. Highlander is an adult kind of organizing training school. It's trying to teach local people how to be leaders of their own movements. And she goes to a two-week workshop. She takes off work to go to this workshop on school desegregation."

In Montgomery at the time, over 50% of the work population were domestic workers who depended on public transportation to go to and from work. African Americans represented 75% of the people who rode the busses. The reaction of the Black community to Rosa Park's arrest was to immediately call for a boycott of the entire Montgomery public bus system. The organizers put together carpools and supported Black-owned gas stations and worked with Black taxi drivers to get people to and from work. This campaign lasted 382 days. In today's dollars, the city of Montgomery lost daily revenue of $3000 per day—that's a total of $1,146,000 dollars.

The Bus Boycott ended December 20, 1956, when the Supreme Court ruled that bus segregation violated the Fourteenth Amendment's equal protection clause.

Jump ahead about six decades. During the COVID-19 global pandemic shut down in Cleveland, Black churches exercised organized people and organized money through GCC. Five of GCC's Black clergy—Rev. Dr. Jawanza Karriem Colvin of Olivet Institutional Baptist Church, Rev. Dr. James P. Quincy, III of Lee Road Baptist Church, Rev. Dr. Lisa Maxine Goods of Shiloh Baptist Church, Pastor Richard Gibson of Elizabeth Baptist Church and Pastor Michele Teague-Humphrey of Imani United Church of Christ--developed the Color of Health Initiative. This initiative focused on the inequity of access to COVID-19 testing and vaccination in predominately Black communities in Cleveland.

We started with calling out the medical redlining by Rite Aid, Walgreens, and CVS pharmacies because they were providing testing in mostly white suburbs but not in the city of Cleveland. Through our organizing work, we got these pharmacies to open up testing in their stores in the city of Cleveland. We also organized seventeen Black churches throughout the city of Cleveland to provide testing to over 5000 people and partnered with United Health Care Insurance Company on their STOP COVID initiative, which became their best and most impactful STOP COVID initiative in the nation.

We then shifted to vaccinations and vaccinated thousands of people in our churches by partnering with the Union of Concerned Scientists Science Democracy Department to teach the science of the vaccines to over a hundred GCC leaders, who then lead small group sessions in their congregations and neighborhoods via Zoom. We worked with Federally Qualified Health Clinics, Ohio State Department of Health, Cuyahoga County Board of Health, and the City of Cleveland Board of Health to bring vaccinations to neighborhoods where our Black congregations hosted mass vaccination clinics every two weeks throughout 2021 and 2022. We pooled our power and our money to leverage our health systems, health insurance corporations, and big pharmacies to be present in our community and to help save lives in low-vaccinated areas.

I am convinced that if we want to make a revolutionary impact for our neighborhoods, the Black churches must think like mediating communities and pool our power, our money, and our people to focus on building broad, big power.

WORLD AS IT COULD BE

As we live and grow as people, at some time in our life journey we learn that the world is *just not fair or just*. The world as it is, right now, is shaped and designed by big business, billionaires, and the politicians (and apparently Supreme Court Justices) they control. They have organized their power, so they win all the prizes. This reality makes me angry and compels me to organize to change it. I have decided to focus my talent and energy working for multi-racial, multi-faith, and multi-class people-power organizations like GCC to help build strong and thriving mediating communities that have the know-how and power to push back and make real change—the kind of hope you can see with your eyes and feel with your hands. The kind of work that can file a grievance and have the power to bring people and their families closer to wholeness.

"The World As It Is" does not match with what we have been taught in our Black congregations to be "The World As It Should Be." We have been taught that we are all made in the image of a God who is almighty and all powerful. So we *must* have this power within us!

As Black churches and other institutions work together to build strong and thriving mediating communities, we will grapple with the tension between the World As It Is and the World As It Should Be to actually create the World As It Could Be. But only if we have enough vision and imagination to organize for power.

⁓⁓⁓

REFLECTION QUESTIONS

1. Give your experiences of the difference between charity and justice.

2. Tell the story about when you first experienced the World As It Is. Have you also experienced the World as It Should Be? If so, tell that story as well.

3. What is your vision of the World As It Could Be? Where did you get that vision?

Part 4

IF THE BLACK CHURCH WANTS JUSTICE

"It's a beautiful day in the neighborhood," said Deacon Alex Hardy of Community Baptist Church as he stood in front of a crowd of over 100 people in September of 2023 who had come to witness the groundbreaking of the new athletic field being built at Washington High School in the Sherman Park community of Milwaukee, Wisconsin.

Washington High School is a historic place. There are several celebrities who attended Washington High School, such as Herb Kohl, former Wisconsin Senator and former owner of the Milwaukee Bucks; Gene Wilder, the late actor and comedian; and Christopher Gardner, businessman and stockbroker whose story was featured in the movie *Pursuit of Happiness*. These are just a few of the famous students who once walked the halls of this school.

As the neighborhood transitioned and families moved from the city to the suburbs, Sherman Park neighborhood changed. It is still a thriving neighborhood in Milwaukee and one of the city's most diverse communities. Replacing the old and dangerous athletic field at Washington High School was a long and hard fight: seven years of meetings, conversations, pushing decision makers to invest in Milwaukee Public School children and the Sherman Park neighborhood. This win started with members of Community Baptist Church; students, faulty, administration at Washington High; and other organizations and residents of the community, all organized by Common Ground (CG), a powerful people's organization in Milwaukee where I was then the Lead Organizer.

CG launched a bold vision in its campaign called "Fair Play": If public dollars will be used to build a new arena for the Milwaukee Bucks, then CG wanted to see at least $150M invested in fixing playgrounds throughout Milwaukee County for children. That campaign launched in the Fall of 2013, and it had several twists and turns; but CG leaders did not quit or give up, they kept pushing. CG negotiated and pushed three Superintendents of the Milwaukee Public Schools: Gregory Thornton, Darienne Driver, and Keith Posley. CG met and talked with Sherman Park members of the Milwaukee City Council, Milwaukee Public School board members, the Milwaukee Bucks President, and local business owners. We outlasted the COVID-19 global pandemic and celebrated a Milwaukee Bucks 2021 National Basketball Association (NBA) championship on the way to raising $2.5M of public and private funds to build a new athletic field at Washington HS. Common Ground made the new facility for Washington High School students and the Sherman Park community a reality.

On September 8, 2023, over 100 CG leaders, Milwaukee Public School Superintendent Keith Posley, and Sherman Park Residents gathered together to break ground for the new athletic field. During this event a young man named Chris, a football player at Washington High school, spoke to the crowd saying, "That field was deadly. You could be running on the field and step in a pothole and break your leg. We had to place tires in different places of the field during practice to avoid stepping in the holes. When I heard the field was going to be fixed, I did not believe it. We are told lots of things, but we never see the results. Standing here today, seeing those bulldozers out there, shows me that it is real, and now I believe it."

The work of leveraging $2.5 million to put in a new athletic field for Washington HS was an example of demanding justice and sticking to the fight until justice comes. And the Black church was in the forefront of the entire effort.

***

In Luke 18:1-8, we are introduced to a familiar New Testament parable. Some call the text the "Persistent Widow" or the "Unjust Judge." I call it "The "Tenacious, Sassy Widow."

The widow was the kind of woman who never gives up and never stops pushing until she gets the justice she deserved. She was bold and smart. She practiced artful disrespect. She did not humble herself in the presence of people with more power or big titles.

When I told my mom I was renaming this text "The Tenacious, Sassy Widow" it caused her to pause. She said, "We do not use that word to describe women in my generation. It's a negative word. A word that was used for a young girl who talked back to adults and sassed them. That kind of behavior got the green switch brought out." Being sassy, said Mom, brought with it serious consequences.

Her response reminded me of a conversation I had with Leon, an older Black man, about how his parents came to Cleveland. He told me, "My mom was from Mississippi, and she was sassy. Her mother had sent her to Cleveland because she was afraid her daughter would be killed because she was so sassy.

Jacquelyn Grant in her book *White Women's Christ and Black Women's Jesus: Feminist Christology and Womanist Response* points out that Black women must navigate between the threefold oppression of racism, sexism, and classism. For Black women, being sassy was dangerous in your home and in your community. Using *sassy* to describe an action of a women and an action that Jesus might praise is a provocative way of thinking about the posture the Black Church could take if we are interested in getting justice for our communities.

Upon deeper reflection of our conversation, my mom came to see that the story of the Tenacious, Sassy Widow is an example of challenging polite and corrupt social norms and being artfully disrespectful to get the justice the widow deserved. In the end, Mom liked the edge and energy of my new title. The qualities of the Tenacious Sassy Widow are the very qualities the Black Church could clothe itself in to address the injustices we see in our community. The text reads:

Now Jesus was telling them a parable to show that at all times they ought to pray and not become discouraged, saying, "In a certain city there was a judge who did not fear God and did not respect *any* person. Now there was a widow in that city, and she kept coming to him, saying, 'Give me justice against my opponent.' For a while he was unwilling; but later he said to himself, 'Even though I do not fear God or respect *any* person, yet because this widow is bothering me, I will give her justice; otherwise by continually coming she will wear me out.'"

And the Lord said, "Listen to what the unrighteous judge said; now, will God not bring about justice for His elect who cry out to Him day and night, and will He delay long for them? I tell you that He will bring about justice for them quickly. However, when the Son of Man comes, will He find faith on the earth?"

Luke 18:1-8 (New American Standard Bible)

Who was this judge? Judges were supposed to be God's representative and ministering justice to those most in need. In 2 Chronicles 19:6-7, we see that as King Josaphat appointed judges in Judah, he instructed them to "consider carefully what you do, because you are not judging for man but for the Lord. For with the Lord our God there is no injustice or partiality or bribery."

The judge in the Sassy Widow parable was not the kind of judge that King Josaphat described. He was the opposite. This judge did not fear God or respect any person. He was not a God-pleaser, nor did he respect the special needs of the poor and the oppressed. This judge was a robber-judge. He was corrupt. He took bribes in the back room. He made decisions based on his own greed. He was bold in his corruption. He had no fear of being made accountable for what judges were *supposed* to be. He did not care about public opinion. If you wanted "justice," you had to pay him, not just a little, but a lot; if you could not pay there was no way you would get the "justice" you deserved. Being a robber-judge was business as usual in Jerusalem.

Who was the widow? Biblical scholars think she was a young woman. Her husband died and she was left alone. In biblical society, women were subjects to the males in their lives. Her husband had given her cover, protection, and the ability to act and move around in the community. When her husband died, she was left vulnerable and alone to fend off the wolves, with no power to fight them off. It was normal for a wife of a deceased husband to have no legal right to inherit her husband's estate. If they had no children, the estate went to her husband's brother, father, or nearest male relative. In this text, the widow was being attacked by an unnamed "opponent" and fighting for her life.

Her husband's estate had been left for other men to try to take it from her. She literally had no recourse but to get the judge to give her justice against her opponent who aimed to take what was hers in justice. The Bible views widows as one of the most vulnerable and helpless members of society, women for whom God has a special concern; we see this in Psalm 68:5 where God is the ultimate defender of widows: "A father of the fatherless and a judge for the widows is God in His holy dwelling."

The woman's unnamed opponent was without doubt some man who had status in his community and the ability to make an *arrangement* with the judge to get the widow's property. "It was not uncommon for unscrupulous executors to leave the widow with nothing," says Jeffrey K. Krehbiel in his book *Reflecting with Scripture on Community Organizing*. "Executors had the status and resources to strike a deal with the judge regarding the estate of a widow's dead husband. This common practice was business as usual." The judges common practice was, according to Rev. Krehbiel, to "dismiss the widow's complaint and strike a deal with the executor. The executor knows this is how things were done, and no one would have expected a different outcome."

But the widow refused to play by the rules of her society. Women were not supposed to be public about being cheated and robbed of their estate. Women were to accept their situation and succumb to the attacks, to give in and walk away according to societal standards and the status quo. Women were to let injustice rule.

Nor could the widow bribe the judge as her opponent could and probably did. She couldn't compete in the back-room negotiations. So she refused to be silent and took her case public in a culture where women had little or no voice. She turned up the heat and kept demanding justice.

In this moment in the story, we see the widow had to make a choice. If she wanted justice, she had to demand it, because the robber-judge was not going to give justice to her. She was in a situation of life or death. She was going to lose everything she and her husband had worked for as a couple.

Now, what would Jesus do or, better yet, what would Jesus have *us* do?

According to the biblical text, the widow kept coming to the robber-judge saying, "Give me justice." She did not cower. She did not give in. She simply kept demanding justice. She would not—could not—take "no" for an answer. She organized a pressure campaign. She was going to get justice or die trying.

She came day in and day out to say to the robber-judge's office, "Give me justice!" "Avenge me!" Maybe she did one of the first "sit-ins" in history!

She followed the robber-judge on the street. She went to his home. Perhaps she showed up in his courtroom. She confronted him in public, where everyone could see. She shined light on her situation in public. She would not relent; she kept coming; she found new ways to force the judge to see and deal with her. Everyone in town knew about her case. Her continued demand for justice probably began to raise the question from the public: "Maybe she *is* being cheated."

The widow finally won. Jesus seemed to approve what she did and even used her as an example of how we should petition the Father in heaven. But the question for us is this: What would Jesus have wanted his own disciples to do to help this tenacious, sassy widow? And, by extension, what would he want the Black Church in the twenty-first century to do to help people in similar situations? Here are five options for Black churches to consider. Which ones would you like your congregation to consider? You can pick none, some, or all of these:

- Pray for people suffering injustice.
- Comfort them.
- Raise money or resources to help them ameliorate the effects of the injustice.
- Help them resolve their individual situation.
- Work to change the system that allows the injustice to continue.

Grappling with these options is the point of this entire book. Often our work of demanding justice makes it necessary to bend the rules. As we see our communities deteriorate while other communities thrive, we see that some rules are made to benefit some while disadvantaging others. It's the theme of public life in some respects.

———

The work of justice does not come quickly. Dr. Martin Luther King reminds us that "the arc of the moral universe is long, but it bends towards justice." The moral arc is bent toward justice by the weight of consistent and persistent effort and organizing, intention and struggle. History shows this in its archives as we see that it took 246 years (1619 to 1865) to end the practice of slavery in the United States. It took the women's suffrage movement 100 years to gain the right for women to vote. It took *another* forty-five years for Black women to organize and win the right to vote.

Black women knew they would only gain their full rights when local and state laws that enforced racial segregation called Jim Crow were abolished, which only happened by passing of the 1965 Voter Rights Act.

It took Common Ground seven years to get $2.5 million to upgrade Washington High School athletic field. In organizing, we do not just wait for justice. Like the tenacious, sassy widow, we organize for justice, we run actions the get reactions from key decision makers, we organize for justice like lives depend on it. Because they do.

In Mark 10:46-52, blind Bartimaeus called out to Jesus even when the disciples tried to silence him. In Luke 8:43-48, the women suffering a non-stop issue of blood for twelve years broke taboos and touched Jesus in public. In Mark 2:1-12, four friends tore off a roof to get their friend healed. In these and so many other cases, Jesus showed a clear preference for tenacious, sassy faith. (If you would like to see this preference dramatized, you might want to watch the popular television series *The Chosen*.)

My friend and editor Greg Pierce, author of *The World as It Should Be: Living Authentically in the Here-and-Now Kingdom of God*, says that even the Good Samaritan would have eventually become a community organizer: "At some point, the Good Samaritan would have tired of picking people out of a ditch and taking them to a hospital. It would have occurred to him that what he needed to do was organize to make the road from Jerusalem to Jericho safe for everyone. That is the act of social justice."

I have come to see the work of organizing as a spiritual discipline of prayer. Organizing is about action, focus, tenacity, and artful disrespect. When the going gets tough, God did not intervene on the widow's behalf; she had to *make* the robber judge act justly.

Jesus did not say *when* justice will come, but he calls us to demand it *until* it comes. Fredrick Douglass' famous quote, "Power concedes nothing without demand, it never has and it never will," is a timeless universal principle of organizing for justice and change.

In organizing, we learn that good ideas and intentions are not enough; they do not move robber-judges or sport-team owners or hesitant politicians. It does not matter if Black churches are "on the side" of the poor and oppressed, they must be willing to organize and fight if they want justice. At least I think that is what Jesus taught. What do you think?

QUESTIONS FOR REFLECTION AND DISCUSSION

1. What is the difference between charity and justice?
2. Which did Jesus preach about it? Cite some chapters and verses!
3. Have you ever helped demand justice for yourself or a loved one or a group of people? How long did you keep at it? What were the results of your demands?

ABOUT THE AUTHOR

Keisha Krumm joined Greater Cleveland Congregations, a nonpartisan community power organization that gives voice and action to social justice issues in Cuyahoga County, Ohio, in November 2019. Keisha came to Greater Cleveland Congregations from its sister organization, Milwaukee-based Common Ground, where she served as Lead Organizer for eight and a half years.

As a veteran organizer, Keisha has built community organizations and developed leaders within congregations, educational associations, nonprofits, and labor unions to tackle issues like voter justice, criminal justice reform, job creation, quality education, affordable physical and mental health care, and racial justice. Keisha has activated thousands of leaders, inspired hundreds of organizers, and her campaigns have led to more than a billion dollars in community investments.

Prior to working at Common Ground, Keisha worked for ten years as an organizer in Los Angeles and the Seattle-Tacoma region. She has a master's degree in Christian Community Development from the Mennonite Brethren Biblical Seminary. She is a devoted wife and mother who has committed her life to justice seeking.

SELECTED BIBLIOGRAPHY

Thurman, Howard. *Jesus and the Disinherited,* Beacon Press, 1976.

Borg, Marcus and Crossan, John Dominic. *The Last Week: A Day-by-Day Account of Jesus's Final Week in Jerusalem,* Harper Collins, 2006.

Rothstein, Richard. *The Color of Law: A Forgotten History of How Our Government Segregated America,* Liveright Publishing Corporation, 2017.

Allen, Danielle. *Our Declaration: A Reading of the Declaration of Independence in Defense of Equality,* Liveright Publishing Corporation, 2015.

BOOKS ON LEADERSHIP

Bending Granite
30+ true stories of leading change
by Tom Mosgaller, et. al.

Ed Marciniak's City and Church
A Voice of Conscience
by Charles Shanabruch

The Heartbeat of Wounded Knee
Native America from 1890 to Present
by David Treuer

Lessons Learned
Stories from a Lifetime in Organizing
by Arnie Graf

Reveille for a New Generation
Organizers and Leaders Reflect on Power
(includes article by Keisha Krumm)
compiled and edited by Greg Pierce

Sometimes David Wins
Organizing to Overcome "Fated Outcomes"
by Frank C. Pierson, Jr.

Song in a Weary Throat
Memoir of an American Pilgrimage
by Pauli Murray

Available from www.actapublications.com
800-397-2282.

BOOKLETS ON COMMUNITY ORGANIZING

Going to the Well to Build Community
A Pastor's Guide to Evangelization
by Timothy E Tilghman

Lessons from One Campaign
for Game-Changing School Reform
by Ramond Domanico

People's Institutions in Decline
Causes, Consequences, Cures and
Effective Organizing for Congregational Renewal
by Michael Gecan

The Power of Relational Action and
Action Creates Public Life
by Ed Chambers

Rebuilding Our Institutions
by Ernesto Cortes, Jr.

How to Raise Money for Your Organization and
Raising Money for Your Congregation
by Robert Connolly

Mixing It Up in the Public Arena
by A. Zeik Saidman

Relentless
Sustaining a Successful People's Campaign
against an Entrenched Public Housing Bureaucracy
by Michael Stanley

Available from www.actapublications.com
800-397-2282.